COPY D̶E̶L̶E̶T̶E̶D̶

November 2023

SPORTS BRANDS

NIKE

BY CARLA MOONEY

Content Consultant
Mark S. Nagel, EdD
Professor, College of Hospitality, Retail
and Sport Management
University of South Carolina

Essential Library
An Imprint of Abdo Publishing
abdobooks.com

ABDOBOOKS.COM

Printed in the United States of America, North Mankato, Minnesota.
052022
092022

THIS BOOK CONTAINS
RECYCLED MATERIALS

Cover Photo: Richard Ulreich/ZUMA Press/CALSP/AP Images
Interior Photos: Optura Design/Shutterstock Images, 4–5; Solari Tienabeso/ Shutterstock Images, 7; Kirby Lee/Alamy, 10; AP Images, 12–13, 14; SOPA Images Limited/Alamy, 16; Piyawat Nandeenopparit/Shutterstock Images, 22; Shutterstock Images, 23, 43, 56–57, 61, 63; Edward Berthelot/Getty Images, 24–25; Ted Shaffrey/ AP Images, 27; Denver Post/Getty Images, 31; Chris Pietsch/AP Images, 35; Dima Gavrysh/AP Images, 36–37; Bob Jordan/AP Images, 39; Beth A. Keiser/AP Images, 41; Revelli-Beaumont/SIPA/SPPFR/AP Images, 48–49; Morry Gash/AP Images, 52; Tina Fineberg/AP Images, 54, 76–77; xMarshall/Alamy, 59; Emilio Andreoli/Getty Images Sport/Getty Images, 66–67; Gareth Copley/PA Images/Alamy, 70; Natalie Behring/ Getty Images News/Getty Images, 73; Peter Charlesworth/Light Rocket/Getty Images, 78; Eric Risberg/AP Images, 83; Craig Ruttle/AP Images, 87; Image of Sport/ Newscom, 89; Gordon Chibroski/Portland Press Herald/Getty Images, 90–91; Xavier Cruells Aguilar/Shutterstock Images, 97

Editor: Arnold Ringstad
Series Designer: Sarah Taplin

Library of Congress Control Number: 2021951584
Publisher's Cataloging-in-Publication Data
Names: Mooney, Carla, author.
Title: Nike / by Carla Mooney.
Description: Minneapolis, Minnesota : Abdo Publishing, 2023 | Series: Sports brands | Includes online resources and index.
Identifiers: ISBN 9781532198137 (lib. bdg.) | ISBN 9781098271787 (ebook)
Subjects: LCSH: Clothing and dress--Juvenile literature. | Nike (Firm)--Juvenile literature. | Sport clothes industry--Juvenile literature. | Brand name products--Juvenile literature.
Classification: DDC 338.7--dc23

CONTENTS

CHAPTER ONE

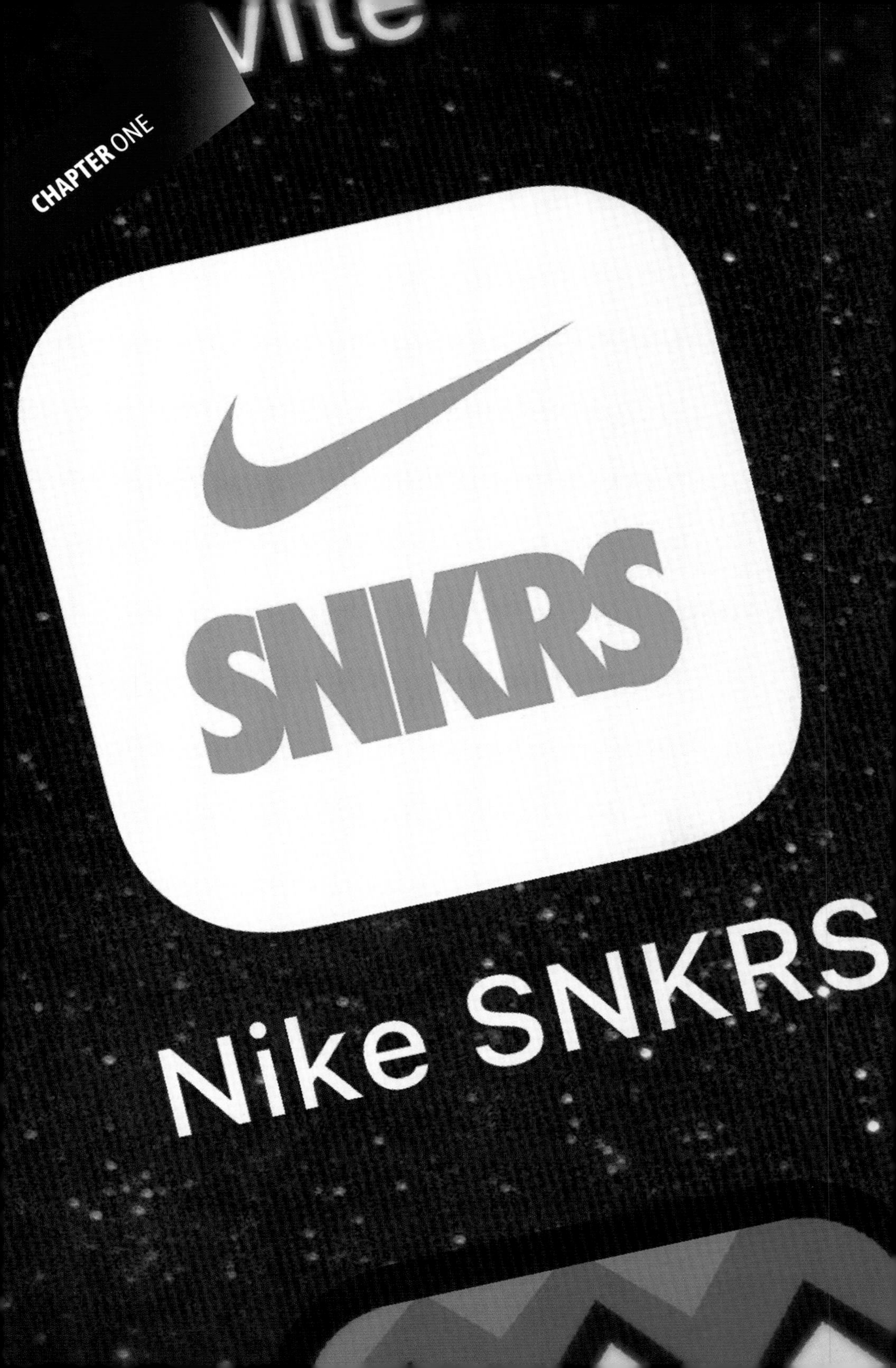

HOT NEW RELEASE

The alarm buzzes in the early morning. It's still a few hours before Simon has to be at work. On any typical day, he'd hit snooze and drift back to sleep. But on this day, he jumps out of bed and grabs his phone. Quickly, he opens Nike's SNKRS app and scrolls to make sure his live Draw entries are in for the Supreme x Nike SB Dunk Low sneakers being released that day.

The live Draw on the SNKRS app is Nike's version of a lottery system. Many of Nike's most sought-after sneaker releases are produced only in limited quantities. Most of the time, the shoes sell out very quickly. As a result, the competition to get them on release day is usually fierce. No longer do customers camp out in a long line

> *Nike's SNKRS app gives devoted fans of the brand a new way to access the company's upcoming product releases.*

outside a store for the chance to buy newly released Nike sneakers. Now, sneakerheads like Simon wait online via the app. The lucky few chosen in the app's lottery are able to buy the limited-edition sneakers that day.

It is not the first time Simon has tried to score a pair of newly released Nike sneakers on SNKRS. He got lucky one time before, scoring a pair of Travis Scott Jordan 4s on the day they dropped. But most of the time, Simon has lost in the lottery. Even so, he keeps trying, and this morning he is glued to his phone. For these shoes, Simon has entered the lottery for each of the four colors being released: Black, Hyper Royal, Mean Green, and Barkroot Brown. He knows from previous experience that the lottery results will be announced one color at a time. Now he impatiently waits and refreshes his screen.

Across the world, hundreds of thousands of people like Simon log on to Nike's SNKRS app to try to score a pair of Nike's hot new shoes.

SNKRS

In 2015, Nike launched its SNKRS mobile app. SNKRS connects users to Nike's shoe releases. It has content about exclusive shoes, a calendar for new releases, and shoes that are currently for sale. Users can set notification reminders for shoe drops that they don't want to miss. Some shoes are released via live Draw, in which users enter for a random chance to purchase. Other times, users can buy shoes via a first-come, first-served system. A SNKRS Pass allows users to reserve a pair of shoes and pick them up in a nearby store.

> *Nike released the Supreme x Nike SB Dunk Low skateboarding sneakers in 2021.*

Some juggle multiple SNKRS accounts or team up with a group of friends to improve their odds of winning the shoe lotteries. Those who don't win are forced to get a pair from aftermarket sites that resell the shoes, often at double or triple the initial lottery price.

Long before the first pair releases, Simon has already set up everything in his account. He filled out his member profile, entered payment info, and typed his shipping address. He wants everything to go smoothly in case he wins the sneaker lottery. Now there is nothing left to do but wait.

Suddenly, Simon's phone vibrates. He looks down and sees the first SNKRS notification. Full of excited anticipation, he swipes and opens it. And there is his first rejection of the day. "Didn't get 'em," says the app about the Black pair. It is disappointing, but Simon knows there are three other colors of the sneaker that he still has a chance to purchase.

A few minutes later, he loses out on the Barkroot Brown pair, and his optimism wavers a bit. Then, he loses out on the Mean Green pair. Now there's only one color left. Simon prepares

SNEAKER COLLECTING

Since the 1980s, sneaker collecting has emerged as a hobby. Sneaker collectors, sometimes called sneakerheads, buy and trade athletic shoes, particularly those made for basketball and skateboarding. The popularity of sneaker collecting can be traced to the release of Nike's wildly popular Air Jordan line of shoes in the mid-1980s. Before long, the signature shoes endorsed by famous athletes became status symbols. For sneaker collectors, the shoes are often more than just something to wear on their feet. While some collectors wear their prized shoes regularly, other collectors never take their shoes outside.

himself for another disappointment as he paces across his bedroom floor.

Then at 9:52 a.m., Simon's phone buzzes with another notification. He opens it and reads: "GOT IT." The Hyper Royal Nikes are his.

A SWOOSH HEARD AROUND THE WORLD

From its humble beginnings in the 1960s, Nike has become a top designer of athletic footwear, apparel, equipment, and accessories for various sports and fitness activities. The company's headquarters are in Beaverton, Oregon, outside of Portland. In 2021, Nike was the world leader in athletic shoes and apparel, reporting $44.5 billion in revenue.[1] In May of that year, the company employed approximately 75,400 people worldwide.[2]

Nike typically hires independent contractors who manufacture its shoes, shirts, hats, and other goods.

NIKE HEADQUARTERS

Nike's headquarters in Beaverton, Oregon, consists of approximately 75 buildings spread across more than 300 acres (120 ha).[3] Some buildings are named after famous Nike-sponsored athletes, including basketball legend Michael Jordan, soccer star Mia Hamm, and runner Steve Prefontaine. Employees can enjoy numerous outdoor features on the campus, including a Japanese garden, two soccer fields, a tennis court, a putting green, and a running trail. If they prefer to stay inside, there are three state-of-the-art fitness centers on campus.

> *Nike's headquarters is located on a sprawling campus in Beaverton, Oregon.*

The company sells its products to customers through several channels, including clothing and shoe stores and its own digital platforms. In addition, the company operates more than 1,000 Nike stores around the world.[4] The company also sponsors many high-profile athletes and sports leagues worldwide, who display its logo on their hats, jerseys, shoes, and more.

In only a few decades, Nike has grown to become one of the most recognizable brands in the world. In 2020, *Forbes* magazine valued Nike's brand at $39.1 billion and ranked the company number 13 on its listing of the most valuable brands in the world.[5]

Nike's logo, the swoosh, is one of the most famous logos on Earth. From athletic competitions to training gyms, tracks, and fields, one can see athletes with apparel or equipment that bears the unmistakable Nike logo. The swoosh appears on shoes, headbands, shirts, uniforms, equipment, and other products. The swoosh has become more than a company logo. Its broad reach is a symbol of Nike's success. Through innovative products and highly effective marketing, Nike has grown from a tiny two-person company into one of the world's most iconic brands.

WHAT IS BRAND IMAGE?

Nike is one of the world's most recognized brands and has a strong brand image. A brand image is a way consumers see a brand based on their interactions with it. Companies such as Nike spend a lot of time and money to build their brand image. They develop a brand personality, voice, and position in the market. All of these factors have a role in how a consumer interacts with and sees a brand. Brand image is important because it affects a company's sales. Customers who identify with a brand image are more likely to buy products and services from that brand.

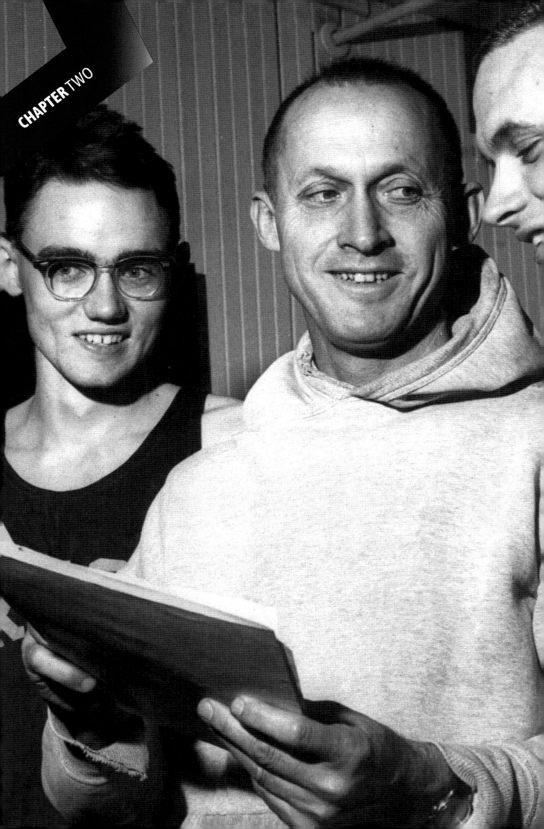

CHAPTER TWO

IN THE BEGINNING

Long before Nike became a household name, it started as the dream of two men in Oregon. In the 1950s, Bill Bowerman was a well-known track-and-field coach at the University of Oregon. Phil Knight was a middle-distance runner on the University of Oregon's track team. Together, Bowerman and Knight put in long hours, hard work, and plenty of inventiveness to turn their dream into a reality.

GETTING STARTED ON THE TRACK

Bowerman was convinced that his college runners could perform better if they just had the right shoes. Using skills he learned from a local shoe cobbler, Bowerman constantly adjusted

> *Bill Bowerman works with two of the University of Oregon's top runners in early 1960.*

13

> *Bowerman*, in hat, *receives a trophy after his Oregon team wins the NCAA championship in 1962.*

and tinkered with different shoe models to find the optimal design. He also experimented with track surfaces and hydration drinks.

Bowerman approached one of his runners, a student named Phil Knight, and asked if he could adjust Knight's shoes with one of his custom designs. Knight agreed. The shoes performed so well that another teammate, Otis Davis, wore them himself. Davis later won two gold medals at the 1960 Summer Olympics in Rome, Italy.

While Bowerman was trying to develop better shoes, Knight was coming up with his own ideas for manufacturing running shoes. At the time, most running shoes sold in the United States came from Germany. As a runner, Knight saw the need for low-priced, quality athletic shoes. After graduating from Oregon in 1959 with a degree in journalism, Knight spent a year in the US Army and then enrolled in Stanford University's master's in business administration program. At Stanford, Knight wrote a paper that explored moving running shoe production from Germany to Japan, where manufacturing labor was less expensive. He sent letters to manufacturers in Japan and elsewhere in Asia proposing his idea but received no response.

BLUE RIBBON SPORTS

After his Stanford graduation in 1962, Knight did not give up on his idea of manufacturing low-priced, quality athletic shoes in Japan. He decided to go to the source and traveled to Japan. There, he contacted a Japanese company, the Onitsuka Tiger company, based in the city of Kobe. Onitsuka manufactured high-quality athletic shoes. Knight made a deal with the company to distribute the company's popular Tiger running shoes in

> *The Onitsuka Tiger brand remains in business today.*

the United States. At the time, running shoes from two German companies, Adidas and Puma, dominated the market. Knight believed demand existed for cheaper, quality-made Tiger shoes in the United States. Knight informally called his venture Blue Ribbon Sports (BRS).

As BRS, Knight received his first shipment of Tiger sample shoes at the end of 1963. At first, he stored the shoes in the basement of his father's house. He drove to track meets in the area and sold pairs of shoes from the trunk of his car. Knight was right in his prediction that there would be demand for the shoes. The shoes sold out in only a few weeks.

Knight also sent Bowerman several pairs of Tiger shoes, hoping to sell a few to his old track coach. However, Bowerman suggested something else. He offered to go into business with Knight as his partner. Together, they officially founded BRS in January 1964 and equally shared ownership of the company. Bowerman invested $500 to match Knight's initial investment.[1] The company's initial strategy was to import Japanese athletic shoes and sell them at a profit in the United States.

In 1964, BRS sold 1,300 pairs of Japanese Tiger running shoes, earning $8,000. The following year, sales rose to $20,000.[2] The company also hired its first full-time employee, Jeff Johnson, another runner at Stanford.

In 1966, BRS rented its first space, located in Santa Monica, California. Now the

BOWERMAN'S HEALTH

Bill Bowerman was Nike's first design innovator, and he spent many hours designing shoes and developing new materials. However, his dedication to innovation damaged his health. Bowerman often worked in a small, poorly ventilated space while using glue and solvents that contained toxic components. Over time, the exposure to toxic materials caused severe nerve damage. Damage to the nerves in his lower legs limited Bowerman's mobility. Eventually, Bowerman was unable to run in the shoes he had designed. Bowerman died in 1999 at the age of 88.

small company's few employees had somewhere to sell shoes other than from their cars. As sales continued to grow, the company opened a distribution office in Wellesley, Massachusetts.

BOWERMAN DESIGNS THE TIGER CORTEZ

Even as BRS sold the Japanese shoes, Bowerman was always thinking about new ways to improve running shoes and a runner's performance. He studied the Tiger shoes and experimented with ways to make them lighter. He used his track athletes to test his designs.

In 1965, Bowerman developed a new shoe design, and he presented it to the Tiger shoe company. Bowerman's design included a cushioned insole. There was soft sponge rubber in the forefoot and the top of the heel, and it had hard sponge rubber in the middle of the heel. The outsole was made of firm rubber. The design became a significant success for Tiger. Named the Tiger Cortez, the shoe went on sale in 1968. Its comfortable, sturdy, and stylish design made the shoe an immediate success.

Bowerman's innovations in shoe design and technology continued. In 1967, he developed a shoe that had its upper portion made of nylon. In 1968, Bowerman and another BRS employee designed the Boston shoe, which featured the first cushioned midsole through the shoe's entire length.

BREAKING UP WITH ONITSUKA

By the end of the 1960s, BRS had reached nearly $300,000 in annual sales. The company expanded into several stores and employed 20 people.[3] The success of BRS and the Tiger Cortez caused increasing strain between BRS and the Onitsuka Tiger company. While distributing the Japanese Tiger shoe, BRS was working on a new line of sneakers. Without telling Onitsuka, BRS had been producing its own version of the Cortez shoe.

When an Onitsuka employee visited BRS's Los Angeles warehouse, the employee discovered the BRS version of the Cortez shoes. Onitsuka accused BRS of selling a competing version of the Tiger Cortez. Knight and Bowerman countered that Onitsuka was trying to get out of their exclusive distribution deal with BRS.

GRASSROOTS MARKETING

When it first started, Blue Ribbon Sports did not have a lot of money for marketing and advertising. Instead, it used grassroots marketing to spread the word about its shoes. Knight personally reached out to runners and showed them his shoes. He convinced them to try the shoes and tell their running friends about them. In this way, word of mouth helped to build interest in BRS shoes.

In 1971, the strain between BRS and Onitsuka became too great to continue the partnership. The two companies formally split. BRS would have to find new factories to produce their shoes. They would also have to choose a new name for their brand.

After the split, Onitsuka filed a lawsuit against BRS. Eventually, a judge ruled that both companies could sell their versions of the Tiger Cortez model. The shoe would become a best-selling model for two different shoe companies. Knight and Bowerman would sell it as the Cortez, while Onitsuka, which eventually became the shoe company Asics, sold it as the Corsair.

NIKE IS BORN

After BRS and the Onitsuka Tiger company ended their distribution deal, Knight and Bowerman decided to rebrand their shoes. At first, Knight suggested the name Dimension Six. However, Jeff Johnson suggested the name Nike after the Greek goddess of victory. "When Jeff Johnson came up with Nike, I didn't know if I liked it too much, but it's better than the other names. It turned out pretty good," said Knight.[4]

Nike brand shoes would also feature a new company logo, the swoosh. The famous logo was created by

Carolyn Davidson, a Portland State University graphic design student. She made the swoosh to represent the wing of the goddess Nike. For her design services, Davidson charged the company $35. It was a small price for a logo that would eventually become recognizable worldwide. At first, Knight did not love the swoosh. "I don't love it, but it will grow on me," he said when Davidson showed it to him.[5] Now that their agreement with Onitsuka Tiger company was done, it was time for Knight and Bowerman to start working on their dream of designing and manufacturing an original brand of athletic shoes.

PREFONTAINE AND NIKE ON THE TRACK

In 1973, Nike signed its first star runner to wear its shoes for $5,000 a year.[6] Oregon native Steve "Pre" Prefontaine was one of the best-known track-and-field athletes in the United States at the time. Pre had been coached by Nike cofounder Bill Bowerman at the University of Oregon. He held several US distance records and ran in the 1972 Summer Olympics in Munich, West Germany. By wearing Nike on the track, Pre helped establish Nike as a trusted brand. He also introduced other track athletes to Nike products, sending personalized notes and shoes to track friends worldwide.

DESIGNING SHOES FOR RUNNERS

N ike has a long history of designing shoes to help runners perform their best. Nike designers consider all of a shoe's elements and how each affects comfort and performance. A shoe's upper is every part that is above the sole. Traditionally, sneaker uppers are made with layers of fabrics and mesh sewn and glued together. Some modern sneakers use knitting technologies to create a single-piece upper that stretches and supports the runner's foot. Nike designers ensure that a sneaker's upper is shaped like a runner's foot and does not bind or chafe anywhere it touches.

Other sneaker features provide support and stability when running. The shoe's heel counter is the part that cradles and supports the runner's heel with each step. The saddle, the reinforced area around the runner's instep, works with the laces to hold the shoe securely to the foot. The toe box holds the shoe's fabric off the runner's toes and protects them from stubbing. Designers work to ensure these features provide the necessary support and protection without binding or rubbing the foot.

In the sole, designers work to provide lightweight cushioning, stability, and support. The sneaker outsole is often made of rubber or foam compounds that provide traction and durability while also being light and flexible. Foam materials between the outsole and the upper cushion the runner from impact forces. Designers also add various technologies such as wedges, medial posts, dual-density foams, and more to add stability. In particular, stability features can prevent the foot from overpronation, or rolling inward.

CHAPTER THREE

EXPANSION AND GROWTH

In 1971, BRS prepared to launch its line of shoes under the brand name Nike. To find factories to make the shoes, Knight traveled to Japan. He met with shoe manufacturers and placed an order for a few thousand shoes, including the Cortez. He ordered several types of athletic shoes for sports such as tennis, basketball, and running. All the shoes would bear the Nike swoosh logo. BRS launched its line of Nike footwear at the 1972 National Sporting Goods Association Show in Chicago, Illinois. At the show, sales reps from around the country got their first look at new athletic products from various companies and could place orders. Knight knew the 1972 show was crucial for the fledgling company. "It was

> *Nike continues to release new versions of its original Cortez shoe today.*

going to be our Super Bowl and our Olympics and our Bar Mitzvah because it was where we'd decided to introduce the world to Nike. If sales reps liked our new shoe, we'd live to see another year. If not, we wouldn't be back for the 1973 show," he said.[1] The sales reps loved Nike shoes, and the orders began to roll in.

In 1972, the US Olympic Team Trials for track and field were held in Eugene, Oregon. It was another opportunity to promote the young company right in its own backyard. Knight sent company reps to Eugene armed with Nike shoes. They passed them out to any athlete willing to take them. Several athletes wore Nike shoes during the trials.

NIKE'S BRIGHT ORANGE BOXES

At the 1972 National Sporting Goods Association Show, Phil Knight wanted a box that would stand out against those of his competitors. At the time, other shoe companies primarily used white or blue boxes. Knight asked Nike's manufacturer to send him boxes that were bright neon orange. He thought it would be the brightest color available. The orange boxes also featured a lowercase "nike" lettered in white on the side of the box.

NIKE MOON SHOES

Meanwhile, Bill Bowerman continued to innovate in his shoe designs. He was consumed with the idea of making running shoes as light as possible. He believed that lighter shoes would give athletes fewer blisters. He was also convinced that athletes would use less energy with more lightweight

An original Nike Moon Shoe was put on display and up for auction in 2019.

shoes, making them faster. At the same time, the shoes needed to have enough grip so that athletes would not slip and fall.

One morning at breakfast, Bowerman considered how to give running shoes more traction without adding weight. As he ate a waffle, Bowerman noticed the waffle's grooves. He wondered what it would look like if the grooves were inverted. Bowerman grabbed the waffle iron to experiment with a new idea for the soles of running shoes. He poured a liquid rubber compound into the waffle iron. After several attempts, Bowerman created a sneaker sole that had grip but was still lightweight. Bowerman's waffle soles became one of Nike's first significant innovations.

In 1972, Bowerman made a prototype of a new running shoe using his waffle sole design. The shoes became known as Nike Moon Shoes. They earned their name because of the waffle-like bottoms, which made impressions on dirt or cinder tracks that looked like the boot prints American astronauts had left on the moon in 1969. Knight filed for a patent on Bowerman's waffle shoe in 1972. The innovative waffle design would become the basis of the company's iconic Nike Waffle Trainer, a running shoe released in 1974.

ATHLETE ENDORSEMENTS

If BRS was going to compete with Adidas, Puma, and other top athletic-shoe brands, it would need professional athlete endorsements. But the company had no idea how to get top athletes to wear and promote its shoes. And it didn't have the money to pay them.

Then Romanian tennis player Ilie Năstase was spotted wearing a new pair of Nike Match Point shoes as he crushed his opponents at the Rainier International Tennis Classic in Seattle, Washington. Knight quickly contacted Năstase's agent and signed the company's first professional athlete endorsement for $10,000.[2] Năstase became the first in a long line of celebrity endorsers.

GROWTH IN THE 1970s

In the 1970s, the popularity of jogging soared across the United States. Demand for Bowerman's Waffle Trainer running shoes spiked. With its unique outer sole, midsole cushioning, and low price, the Nike Waffle Trainer attracted thousands of new customers to the Nike brand. Its traction and cushioning were better than any other running shoe on the market and helped create a loyal customer following.

In 1974, BRS opened its first US manufacturing plant, in Exeter, New Hampshire. By the end of the year, sales approached $5 million. The company continued the aggressive promotion of its brand and shoes. BRS recruited more athletes, including tennis player Jimmy Connors, to wear Nike shoes.

In 1976, the Olympic Trials for track and field were again held in Eugene, Oregon.

HOLLYWOOD WEARS NIKES

In the 1970s, BRS distributed Nike shoes to aspiring and established Hollywood stars. Before long, Nike shoes appeared on television. Characters in hit shows such as *Starsky & Hutch*, *The Six Million Dollar Man*, and *The Incredible Hulk* appeared on-screen wearing Nike shoes. In a 1977 episode of *Charlie's Angels*, popular actor Farrah Fawcett wore a pair of Nikes. A single television shot of Fawcett wearing the shoes caused them to sell out in every store across the country by noon the following day. The Hollywood exposure helped to drive the demand for Nike shoes even higher.

Athletes wearing Nike shoes turned in impressive performances. At the 1976 Olympic Games in Montréal, Québec, Canada, several athletes in high-profile events wore Nike shoes. That year, Nike's revenue rose to $14 million. It had doubled to $28 million by 1978.[3] To keep up with the demand for its shoes, BRS added overseas manufacturing facilities in Taiwan and South Korea. It also expanded its product line and added athletic shoes for children.

Around this time, Knight noticed that athletic sneakers were expanding beyond sports activity into everyday life. He wondered if people might start wearing sneakers off the track and into classrooms, offices, and other everyday settings. That gave him the idea to make the popular Waffle Trainer in blue to look good with jeans. He recalled:

> We couldn't make enough. Retailers and sales reps were on their knees, pleading for all the Waffle Trainers we could ship. The soaring pair counts were transforming our company, not to mention the industry. We were seeing numbers that redefined our long-term goals, because they gave us something we'd always lacked—an identity. More than a brand, Nike was now becoming a household word, to such an extent that we would have to change the company name.[4]

> *Running recreationally was a new concept during the late 1970s, and Nike came to dominate the market.*

In 1978, Blue Ribbon Sports officially changed its name to Nike Inc. By 1979, the company was selling nearly half the running shoes in the United States.

SMALL STEPS IN ADVERTISING

In 1976, BRS hired its first advertising agency. The Seattle, Washington, firm John Brown and Partners would help market the growing company. The following year, the agency created Nike's first ad campaign. It featured the slogan "There is no finish line." The ad featured a single runner on an empty country road lined with tall Douglas fir trees. The ad's copy read: "Beating the competition is relatively easy. Beating yourself is a never-ending commitment."[5] The ad did not focus on Nike's shoes but rather on the spirit of the company. It was unlike other ads at the time.

Still, Knight remained skeptical about the value of advertising. "A product, I thought, speaks for itself, or it doesn't. In the end, it's only quality that counts. I couldn't imagine that any ad campaign would ever prove me wrong or change my mind," he said.[6]

AIR DESIGN

In 1977, former aerospace engineer M. Frank Rudy and his business partner, Bob Bogert, met with Nike executives. They wanted to pitch a new idea for running shoes. Rudy explained that he had developed a way to inject air into the shoe's soles, providing greater support and cushioning.

At first, Knight was skeptical. Then he heard that Adidas had passed on the technology. "Abracadabra. That was all I needed to hear," said Knight.[7] He took the air soles for a test run. When he got back, he was convinced they had great potential. The company signed a deal with Rudy and Bogert to develop the technology for their shoes.

The first shoe to feature the air technology was the 1978 Nike Tailwind running shoe.

GOING PUBLIC

Despite its initial successes, Nike still needed more cash to grow its product offerings and marketing efforts. The obvious solution was to make a public stock offering and sell shares of the company to the public. Yet Knight resisted. He feared that selling public shares would change Nike. He was also afraid that his team would lose control of the company.

Eventually, Knight could no longer deny the need to finance Nike's growth. He agreed to the public stock offering. In December 1980, Nike issued two million shares of stock available for the public to purchase. This stock sale allowed Nike to raise the money it needed to grow. It was

TAILWIND MISCUE

At the end of 1978, Nike released its first sneaker that featured air sole technology, the Tailwind. The shoe launched with a splashy ad campaign and a lot of hype. In the first ten days, sales took off. Then, reports began to surface about a problem with the shoes. Customers returned the Tailwind to stores. They complained the shoes were falling apart. Analysis of the returned shoes uncovered a design flaw. Tiny bits of metal in the shoe's silver paint rubbed against the shoe's upper part, slicing and shredding the fabric. Nike offered full refunds to its customers. Approximately half of the Tailwind shoes landed in recycling bins.

also structured so that Knight and Bowerman would retain control of the company.

With the money to fund growth, Nike charged into the 1980s with aggressive marketing and expansion. Throughout the decade, Nike expanded its product lines. When enthusiasm for jogging began to decline in the United States in the early 1980s, the company focused on other types of athletic shoes, such as basketball and tennis shoes. New product lines in apparel, leisure shoes, and children's shoes also performed well.

Nike expanded overseas too. It formed Nike International Ltd. in 1981 to launch the company's moves into Europe, Asia, Latin America, and Africa. During the 1980s, Nike transformed from a US shoe distributor to a worldwide brand.

ACQUISITIONS

Since its founding, Nike has acquired other shoe, sporting equipment, and athletic apparel companies. These acquisitions have allowed Nike to diversify its product line. In 1988, Nike purchased footwear company Cole Haan. It followed that acquisition with purchases of Bauer Hockey (1994), surf apparel company Hurley International (2002), shoe company Converse (2003), athletic apparel company Starter (2004), and sports equipment company Umbro (2008). In the late 2000s, Nike decided to sell off some of its subsidiaries to refocus its business. By 2020, only Converse remained as a key Nike subsidiary.

> *Knight waved to fans at a 2014 basketball game at the University of Oregon, where he has become a beloved figure.*

INNOVATION, MARKETING, AND GROWTH

In the 1990s, Nike moved into its world headquarters campus in Beaverton. The company opened NikeTown stores in the United States and overseas, including in Germany and England. Nike has remained dedicated to innovation, marketing, and expansion into new markets.

In 2016, cofounder Phil Knight retired from his position as the chairman of Nike's board of directors. Under his leadership, Nike had become a global phenomenon with more than $32 billion in annual revenue.[8] Nike's portfolio now includes a large variety of sports, including baseball, cricket, golf, football, tennis, and many more.

CHAPTER FOUR

A MARKETING MASTER

T oday, Nike is one of the world's most recognizable brands. Its brand recognition is partly due to the distinctive swoosh logo on every Nike product. Nike has also created some of the world's most memorable and emotion-generating ad campaigns. Using simple slogans and compelling messages, Nike captures the attention and imagination of people worldwide.

EARLY CAMPAIGNS

Before the 1980s, Nike primarily used endorsements from athletes and small print ads in magazines to market its products. By the 1980s, Nike sought to reach more potential customers. Its sales were slowing, and competitors such as Reebok were making

> Tennis star Maria Sharapova films an ad for Nike in 2006. Collaborations with elite athletes have become a key part of Nike's marketing strategy.

37

gains in the athletic shoe and apparel market. It was time for Nike to put more emphasis on its advertising.

Phil Knight met with the ad agency Wieden+Kennedy. Knight was skeptical about advertising. However, Dan Wieden, the agency president, soon changed Knight's mind.

Wieden+Kennedy believed that Nike could win more consumers if it created a campaign around a sport that was rapidly growing in popularity, basketball. The agency suggested that Nike sponsor a basketball player who could be a brand ambassador and a central figure in an advertising campaign. They recommended that Nike look for a young, rising player, someone on the verge of becoming a basketball superstar.

A young player named Michael Jordan seemed like a perfect fit. Jordan had been a star player from the University of North Carolina and helped the Tar Heels win the national title in 1982. He also led the American men to a gold medal in the 1984 Summer Olympics. In June 1984, the Chicago Bulls selected Michael Jordan in the National Basketball Association (NBA) Draft. There was one problem. Jordan wanted to sign an endorsement deal with his favorite basketball shoe company, Adidas.

Nike saw enormous potential in Michael Jordan as an endorser for its products.

Nike consultant Sonny Vaccaro, who had helped promote Nike's shoes among college teams, persuaded Nike that Jordan would be their best choice for a college player to sign. When Jordan met with Vaccaro and Nike executives, they convinced him to go with Nike. The company's emphasis on innovation impressed Jordan. And Nike promised to make a custom-fit shoe for him, which had never been done for a basketball shoe before. It also pledged to run a million-dollar advertising campaign around Jordan's new Nike basketball shoe. Jordan signed the deal.

BANNED ON THE COURT

In October 1984, Nike launched the basketball shoe that it had made for Jordan. The NBA banned the shoe because its black and red colors did not match the shoes of Jordan's Chicago teammates. Every time Jordan wore the shoes in a game, the NBA fined him $5,000.[1] Nike paid the fines for Jordan because the media attention was much more valuable. Next, Nike launched a television commercial to advertise the banned basketball shoes. People rushed to buy the Nike shoes worn by the impressive rookie who could seemingly fly across the basketball court.

In 1985, Nike created the Air Jordan 1 shoe. Priced at $65, the Air Jordan 1 was one of the most expensive basketball shoes on the market.[2] Wieden+Kennedy created an advertising campaign for the Air Jordan 1 that included a television commercial starring Jordan himself. The creative commercial was filmed in slow motion and

> *With his incredible slam dunks, Jordan lived up to the Air Jordan brand's name.*

featured Jordan driving to the net, sailing through the air, and slam-dunking a basketball. Fans took notice.

Nike's creative marketing and Jordan's phenomenal talent were a winning combination. In his first NBA season, Jordan averaged 28.2 points per game and won the Rookie of the Year Award. Jordan was on his way to becoming a basketball legend and eventual Hall of Famer. He would go on to win six NBA championships, five Most Valuable Player Awards, ten scoring titles, and many more awards.[3] Nike sold $100 million worth of Air Jordan shoes in just the first year.[4] It was the beginning of a long and very successful partnership that would become a multibillion-dollar business.

"REVOLUTION"

In 1987, Nike first aired "Revolution," a black-and-white commercial that changed advertising. Before this ad, most ads used original jingles or covers of popular songs. In this commercial, Nike used the real version of the Beatles' song "Revolution." By using the real version, Nike opened the door for commercials to use original songs performed by the artists who made them famous to market everything from shoes to phones. At the time, the surviving members of the Beatles were not happy and sued Nike. Ultimately, the case was settled out of court.

"JUST DO IT"

The ads for the Air Jordan represented just the beginning of Nike's marketing innovation. In the 1980s, Nike's

> *With "Just Do It," Nike gained a world-famous slogan to go with its renowned logo.*

competitor, Reebok, was still doing more shoe business than Nike. Nike needed something new to help it stand out.

In 1988, Nike debuted a new marketing campaign with the slogan "Just Do It." The very first commercial featured elderly marathon runner Walt Stack. A shirtless Stack wearing Nike shoes ran across the Golden Gate Bridge in San Francisco, California, while upbeat music played. Stack declared that he ran 17 miles (27 km) every day and joked about how his teeth didn't chatter in the cold because he kept them in his locker. Then, the new slogan appeared on the screen: "Just Do It."[5]

Nike hoped its campaign would appeal to everyone, not just the fittest athletes. By choosing an elderly runner to feature in its ad, Nike stood out from the competition. Pairing the likable Stack with the "Just Do It" slogan was meant to inspire and motivate potential Nike customers on the other side of the television screen. The advertising campaign was a big hit. "Just Do It" became the company's signature slogan and is still used today. Dean DeBiase, an expert in advertising and brand strategy, explains:

> Nike has always positioned itself as the essence of what drives the athletes and those who want to be more active, and uniquely understands the emotional motivation and reward of doing so. Its "Just Do It" campaign epitomizes this. It embodies both the exhilaration and the challenges of competition and fitness. It speaks directly to the emotions of athletes.[6]

"BO KNOWS"

Innovative advertising continued to be an essential part of Nike's marketing strategy. In 1989, the company needed to generate excitement for its new cross-training shoe. Ad executive Jim Riswold proposed designing a campaign around Bo Jackson, a multisport athlete who played professional baseball for the Kansas City Royals and professional football for the Los Angeles Raiders. His excellence in both sports made him an ideal choice to endorse cross-training sneakers suited for any activity.

During the 1989 Major League Baseball (MLB) All-Star Game, Nike debuted its "Bo Knows" ad campaign. The ads featured quick shots of Jackson trying his hand at everything from basketball to golf while famous Nike-sponsored athletes such as tennis player John McEnroe and Michael Jordan talked about how "Bo knows" their sport. The campaign generated attention and sales as the "Bo Knows" slogan appeared in print ads, in television commercials, and on T-shirts.

MICHAEL JORDAN & MARS BLACKMON

In 1988, Nike created a series of memorable ads starring Michael Jordan and his sidekick, Mars Blackmon. Mars Blackmon was a fictional character from the film *She's Gotta Have It*, played by Spike Lee, the film's writer and director. Lee's appearance in the Nike ads gave more credibility to the Air Jordan line of shoes. It paved the way for the Nike shoes to go beyond sportswear and become part of urban and pop culture.

"IF YOU LET ME PLAY"

One of Nike's most memorable ad campaigns focused on positioning the brand as meaningful for women. In the fall of 1995, Nike debuted a 30-second TV spot, "If You Let Me Play," in prime time. The powerful ad took a new approach to inspire female athletes by featuring young girls quoting statistics on the benefit of sports in girls' lives. Along with featuring women on-screen, the commercial was also written and produced by women.

Maureen O'Connor, director of Portland State University's advertising program, remembers the Nike women's campaign. "That original Nike women's campaign spoke to a lot of women (like me). . . . We didn't have much opportunity to play sports, even if we wanted to. Nike told us it wasn't too late for us, and it surely wasn't too late for our daughters," she said.[7]

"FIND YOUR GREATNESS"

In 2012, Nike launched a global ad campaign called "Find Your Greatness." The ad focused on everyday athletes. It featured a young boy jogging down an empty rural road while wearing Nike gear. Over the powerful scene, a voice talked about finding greatness in everyone. The boy in the commercial was not a famous athlete, but he found his personal greatness as he jogged down the lonely road.

The emotional ad spoke to the audience and told them that Nike's products were not just made for elite athletes. Instead, Nike is for anyone and everyone who strives toward a goal. Like many of Nike's most enduring commercials, "Find Your Greatness" highlighted the brand's inclusive stance toward all types of people.

BUILDING A BRAND IDENTITY

Nike's decades-long partnership with Wieden+Kennedy has produced some of the most memorable and influential marketing campaigns in retail history. Many of the campaigns do not focus on just one Nike product. Instead, some of the company's best marketing campaigns and ads highlight Nike as a brand.

Marketing has allowed Nike to create a strong brand identity. Consumers can identify with the company through its advertising messages. These people can further promote Nike brand awareness both through social media and in person, helping to grow a network of passionate consumers who are loyal to Nike and its products.

CHAPTER FIVE

PROMOTING NIKE

Over the years, Nike has spent billions of dollars on sponsorships and endorsements. Much of this money has gone to endorsement deals with athletes, including superstars such as Michael Jordan and LeBron James. "For as long as Nike has been around, the face of the organization has been these high-profile athletes. It's part of their DNA," says David Carter, executive director of the University of Southern California's Sports Business Institute.[1] In addition to professional athletes, Nike also sponsors leagues, teams, and college athletic programs.

Nike's decision to spend so much money on athlete endorsements is important in its overall marketing strategy.

> *Jordan attended a press conference in Paris in 2015 to celebrate the thirtieth anniversary of his Nike brand.*

When top athletes and celebrities promote a product, people tend to listen more than they would if an unknown actor starred in an ad. Some of Nike's most enduring and memorable marketing campaigns have featured star athletes who are recognized worldwide.

The ultimate goal of endorsements and sponsorships is to sell more products. Fans who see their favorite athletes or teams wearing Nike gear are more likely to go out and buy Nike for themselves. A study published by the Marketing Science Institute found that after Nike signed an endorsement deal with golfer Tiger Woods in 1996, the Nike golf ball division alone increased profits by $103 million between 2000 and 2010.[2] When choosing athletes to sponsor, Nike tends to approach men and women who are doing very well in their sports and have a great fan following. They search for athletes who are passionate about their sports and who can

CELEBRITY COLLABORATIONS

Along with athlete endorsements, Nike has also partnered with influential celebrities to promote the brand. For example, pop singer Justin Timberlake has collaborated with Nike for several shoe designs. In 2018, Nike announced the release of a new collaboration with Timberlake, the Air Jordan III JTH. The shoe's design was inspired by a song from Timberlake's *Man of the Woods* album. Excerpts from the song's lyrics are featured on the shoe insoles. Collaborating with celebrities helps Nike promote its brand with people who are into style more than sports.

be people fans look up to. By recruiting up-and-coming athletes, the company hopes to find the next Michael Jordan, a player with the talent and charisma to excel both in his or her sport and in marketing for Nike products.

NIKE'S ICONIC ATHLETES

Starting in 1984, Michael Jordan and Nike teamed up for one of the most iconic endorsement deals in history. While Jordan starred in many ad campaigns, one of the most memorable came in the late 1990s. It featured him talking about all the failed shots and lost games he had experienced. He said the failures had helped to build him into the athlete he eventually became.

Golf superstar Tiger Woods is another one of Nike's most famous athletes. In 1996, Nike signed Woods to represent Nike shoes shortly after the young golfer turned professional. Nike built a line of golf-related products around Woods in the following years, which continued until the company stopped making golf clubs and bags in 2016 to focus on apparel. At every golf tournament, Woods can be seen wearing Nike shoes and clothing. He has starred in numerous ad campaigns for the company. One of the most memorable ads featured the golfer

> *Woods sports a Nike cap in 1996, the same year the company signed him as an endorser.*

balancing and juggling a golf ball on his club before hitting it down the range.

Nike has also signed many female athletes across a variety of sports to endorsement deals. These women include tennis star Maria Sharapova, soccer player Alex Morgan, snowboarder Chloe Kim, and soccer star

Megan Rapinoe. One of Nike's most famous female partners is tennis superstar Serena Williams. In 2003, Nike signed Williams to a multiyear sponsorship contract. At the time, Williams was already a star on the tennis court, having won several Grand Slam titles. She would continue her dominance on the court and go on to win 23 Grand Slam singles titles through 2021, more than any other player in modern tennis.[3] One of Williams's most memorable ad campaigns with Nike, released in 2019, was called "Dream Crazier." The commercial featured pro and amateur athletes in action while Williams narrated an empowering message to female athletes.

In 2003, an 18-year-old basketball player named LeBron James signed a seven-year, $90 million endorsement deal with Nike.[4] James was selected first overall in the 2003 NBA Draft by the Cleveland Cavaliers. He was one of the most anticipated basketball players in years. Nike beat out other shoe companies to sign James and add him to a lineup of star athletes that included big name basketball players Shaquille O'Neal and Allen Iverson. They had placed a bet on James's potential, and that bet ended up paying off massively. Over his career, James has become one of the greatest and most famous basketball players of all time.

> *In 2003, fans lined up to purchase Nike's LeBron James shoes.*

UNIFORM AND EQUIPMENT DEALS

In addition to sponsoring individual athletes, Nike also relies on partnerships with teams and leagues as part of its global marketing strategy. Making deals to supply uniforms and equipment to teams and leagues gives Nike exposure to a worldwide audience. Every time a team wearing Nike takes the field, the iconic swoosh flashes in the stadium, on television, and in media coverage.

In the United States, Nike has partnered with the National Football League (NFL), the NBA, and MLB to provide uniforms. In 2018, Nike and the NFL extended their partnership through 2028. The agreement states that Nike will supply all 32 NFL teams with game-day uniforms and sideline apparel. Nike will also provide additional gear to NFL players with individual sponsorship contracts, including Seattle Seahawks quarterback Russell Wilson. "Nike has been a longtime and trusted partner of [the] NFL and we're thrilled to extend our relationship with them," said Brian Rolapp, the NFL's chief media and business officer.[5]

In some cases, sponsored athletes have made news not for their athletic achievements but for misdeeds in their personal lives. As a result, Nike sometimes has to limit athlete ad exposure for a time or even potentially cancel partnership agreements with athletes involved in scandals to protect the Nike brand from negative associations. In other cases, Nike stands by athletes who have been accused of bad behavior.

Around the world, Nike also has uniform supplier deals in soccer, partnering with teams worldwide, including Barcelona, Chelsea, Liverpool, and Inter Milan. Uniform deals for these clubs placed the company and its brand in front of customers in major European cities such as London, Paris, and Barcelona. In the 2019–2020 season, Nike spent an estimated $356 million on uniform supplies for English, French, German, Italian, and Spanish soccer leagues.[6] Nike's endorsements with athletes and partnerships with leagues and teams have solidified it as one of the most recognizable brands in the world.

NIKE'S FAMILY OF PRODUCTS

Since its early days as a small athletic-shoe company, Nike has expanded into a wide range of products. It carries not only shoes but also apparel, accessories, and equipment for a wide variety of leisure activities. It has become one of the world's largest sports brands.

ATHLETIC SHOES

Athletic shoes remain a significant part of the company's sales. For the fiscal year ending in May 2021, Nike had global footwear sales of $28 billion. This made up nearly two-thirds of the company's total revenue.[1]

Nike's footwear products are primarily designed for athletic use. Nike has specific lines of footwear for a wide

> Nike's stores around the world now carry far more than the shoes that gave the company its start.

variety of activities, such as basketball, football, soccer, running, and volleyball. Its highest-selling shoe categories are running, basketball, and soccer. In addition to athletic shoes, Nike also sells footwear for more casual use. Its lifestyle line of footwear is designed to be comfortable for everyday wear.

MAKING NIKE PRODUCTS

Nike products are made in 41 countries around the world, including Argentina, Bangladesh, Cambodia, China, Ecuador, India, Malaysia, Thailand, and the United States. All of Nike's products are made by independent contractors, and Nike does not own any of the factories. All footwear and apparel products are made overseas, while equipment products are made both in the United States and overseas. This approach has helped Nike reduce manufacturing and inventory costs.

APPAREL

Beyond shoes, Nike sells apparel for men, women, and children. In 2021, Nike apparel sales made up 31 percent of the company's total revenue.[2] Nike apparel products include T-shirts, shorts, sweatshirts, hoodies, pants, tights, jackets, vests, swimwear, polo shirts, yoga wear, socks, underwear, sports bras, and leggings. Nike even has a line of maternity clothes for pregnant women. Much of Nike's apparel is designed for use in specific athletic and recreational activities. If a person needs a shirt for running or padded shorts for cycling, Nike sells them. Nike also

AIR MAX 1

I n 1987, Nike introduced the Air Max 1, a running sneaker that featured visible air technology. During a visit to Paris, France, Nike designer Tinker Hatfield was inspired by the inside-out architecture of the Centre Pompidou. The building's structure features visible plumbing, air ducts, and wiring on the outside of the building. Hatfield pushed Nike to make a shoe with its inner workings visible on the outside. He cut a small window into the sneaker's sole that revealed the shoe's air bag cushioning, a urethane air bag filled with pressurized gas. Early sketches of Hatfield's idea were not well received, and some people at Nike believed he should be fired. However, Hatfield persuaded the company to give his idea a chance. They did, and the trailblazing Air Max 1 was a hit. Over the years, the Nike Air Max 1 has become one of the most famous designs in Nike history.

produces apparel that features licensed logos from college teams, professional teams, and leagues.

ACCESSORIES AND EQUIPMENT

Nike sells accessories and equipment for a variety of sports and recreational activities. People can buy Nike equipment for specific sports, such as soccer balls, swim goggles, and yoga mats. The company also sells products to use for other activities, including hats, visors, and water bottles. Sales of accessories and equipment are a much smaller part of Nike's overall business than footwear and apparel. In the fiscal year ending in May 2021, equipment and accessories made up 3 percent of the company's total revenue.[3]

Some of these products now incorporate advanced technology. Nike has partnered with tech giant Apple to produce a Nike-branded version of the Apple Watch.

The Apple Watch Nike features an exclusive Nike sports band. It runs the Nike Run Club app, which uses a built-in GPS sensor to track a runner's pace, distance, and route. The app also provides users with motivation and coaching plans. "We know runners—and we know many are looking for a device that gives them an easy, fun way to start running," said president of the Nike brand Trevor Edwards in 2016. "The market is full of complex, hard-to-read devices that focus on your data. This focuses on your life. It's a powerful device with a simple solution— your perfect running partner."[4]

STREET FASHION

The Nike brand has extended beyond sports to become a fashion status symbol in many places. Starting in the 1980s, certain Nike clothing items and shoes became fashionable for American youth. In particular, young people sought out Nike tracksuits, baseball caps, and certain brands of shoes—in particular the Air Jordan, Air Force 1, and Air Max brands. They wore these Nike products as part of their casual, everyday wear.

Sneaker media expert Russ Bengtson points to the timeless Nike Air Jordan 1, released in 1985, as the shoe that helped Nike become a fashion statement:

> Until the Nike Air Jordan, basketball shoes were primarily marketed to—and sought out by—basketball players. Air Jordan changed all that. As much of a standout on store shelves as it was on NBA courts, the first Air Jordan became a universal status symbol like no other sneaker before it. Jordan wore it, yes, but so did [rapper] LL Cool J and the coolest kid in your class. This was when sneakers went from 'want' to 'need.'[5]

Today, the popularity of Nike apparel and footwear as street fashion has continued to grow. Young people around the world style Nike sneakers, leggings, sweatpants, and tracksuits with other casual clothing

AIR FORCE 1

The Air Force 1 has become Nike's best-selling sneaker of all time. It is an impressive achievement for a shoe that was intended to be a limited release. In 1982, Nike released the original Air Force 1, a basketball sneaker designed by Nike product designer Bruce Kilgore. The shoe included Nike Air technology, which used pressurized air in a tough, flexible bag in the shoe's sole. The air technology provided flexible cushioning while keeping the shoes lightweight. The Air Force 1 also featured a high-top design and a circular sole to withstand intense action and maintain grip on the court. Nike discontinued production of the Air Force 1 in 1984. But people still wanted the shoes. When they could not find new Air Force 1s, some people began to customize older Air Force 1s by adding colors. The increasing demand convinced Nike to reintroduce the shoe in 1986. Over the years, Nike has released the shoe in new colors and models. Millions of people around the world love the Air Force 1 for its style and comfort.

pieces. They wear Nike basketball socks as a fashion statement and seek out exclusive sneaker releases so they can wear the latest Nike status symbols.

SELLING TO CUSTOMERS

Nike uses several methods to sell its products to customers. Some products are sold through dealer networks, which include footwear stores and chains, department stores, sporting goods stores, athletic specialty stores, and other retail merchants. Nike merchandise is also sold directly to customers through Nike stores. In 2021, the company operated more than 1,000 retail stores worldwide. In the United States, there were more than 300 Nike stand-alone stores.[6] These included Nike-brand stores, Nike Factory stores, and Converse stores.

Nike also reaches customers directly through its website. Launched in 1999, the website's online store allows customers to research products from shoes to shorts to hats. Once they have found the items they want, customers can purchase them online and Nike will ship them directly to their homes.

Nike customers can also shop directly on the company's mobile apps, the Nike app, and the SNKRS app.

The apps have proved to be popular with customers. In the last quarter of Nike's fiscal year 2021, 40 percent of Nike's online direct sales came from its mobile apps. In particular, the SNKRS app, which lets customers buy limited-edition Nike sneakers earlier than other shoppers, had 90 percent more members than the previous year.[7]

In 2021, online sales made up 21 percent of Nike's total direct-to-customer revenue.[8] The company expects this percentage to keep growing in the future as it focuses on growing its digital business. "There is a fundamental shift in consumer behavior toward digital. . . . And that provides the opportunity for us to have a direct connection with consumers, " said Nike Chief Executive Officer John Donahoe in 2021.[9]

CONVERSE

Nike acquired the American shoe company Converse in 2003. Founded in 1908, Converse is well known for its footwear, apparel, and accessories. In 1917, the company introduced its now famous Converse All Star basketball shoes. Converse chose Charles H. "Chuck" Taylor to be its brand ambassador. Taylor was a basketball player for the Akron Firestone Non-Skids. In 1921, he joined the Converse sales team and traveled around the country promoting the All Star shoe at basketball clinics. In 1932, Converse added Taylor's signature to the All Star patch on the high-top sneakers.

CHAPTER SEVEN

HIGH-TECH DESIGN

Throughout the years, Nike has focused on creating quality products that help athletes perform better. Whether it be Bill Bowerman experimenting with a waffle iron or research scientists analyzing data in the Nike Sport Research Lab, Nike's focus on design, research, and development is one of the key reasons it has become one of the world's leading athletic-shoe and apparel companies.

NIKE SPORT RESEARCH LABORATORY

In the late 1970s, a running boom spread around the United States. Soon after, in 1980, Nike's first research lab was established in Exeter, New Hampshire. Nike created the research

> *Nike researcher Geng Luo showed off an advanced new design at a 2017 press conference.*

lab to understand the needs of runners better so it could make the best products for athletes.

Today, much of Nike's research and design work occurs at the Nike Sport Research Laboratory (NSRL) in Beaverton, Oregon. The enormous NSRL brings together athletes, researchers, and designers to develop the latest Nike products. "The NSRL is the epicenter of where we work with athletes of all abilities, all backgrounds, all skills, and all sports," says the lab's Matthew Nurse, PhD.[1]

At the NSRL, researchers study athletes such as soccer star Megan Rapinoe and marathon runner Eliud Kipchoge. To gain valuable information, they record all types of metrics, from differences in feet to the amount of force applied when athletes' feet hit the ground. The researchers use this information to create guidelines for product engineers when designing apparel and footwear to improve performance. At the NSRL, athletes also train under the eye of Nike scientists. The collaboration allows the

NIKE FLYKNIT

Just in time for the 2012 Summer Olympics in London, England, Nike unveiled its newest shoe technology, Nike Flyknit. This is a digitally engineered knitting process that creates seamless, formfitting, and lightweight shoe uppers. It allows the Flyknit to wrap smoothly around the athlete's entire foot, which helps him or her to feel more secure and in control when moving. The result is a light, breathable shoe that provides a second-skin-like fit.

athletes to learn more about themselves and their bodies, which can improve their performance.

Nike's research is not limited to elite athletes. It also studies everyday people who run on neighborhood streets or play pickup basketball. According to Nurse, approximately 80 to 85 percent of people who come to the NSRL are everyday athletes with different backgrounds and body types. By studying these active people, Nike can learn quickly and develop better products faster.

GETTING A BASELINE

Thousands of athletes come to the NSRL each year. When they arrive, they fill out a digital survey. It asks questions about what kinds of activities or sports they do. It also inquires about their goals, motivations, and preferences. The survey asks about the products they have used, as well as what their future needs might be. Next, each athlete completes several physical baseline tests. Among the tests, athletes undergo a 3D laser scan of the foot, a foot pressure test, a vertical jump test, and a full-body scan.

These baseline tests allow Nike to evaluate the athletes and better understand them. The testing data also goes into a global database used in the design and fit

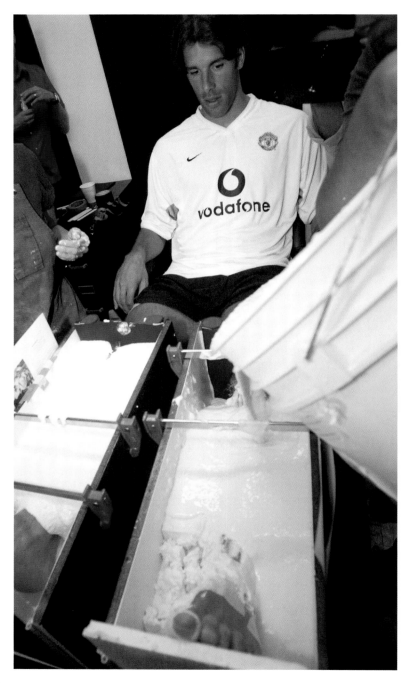

> *Soccer player Ruud Van Nistelrooy had casts of his legs made at the NSRL.*

of Nike products. The insights researchers gain from these tests help them create new technologies for Nike's latest footwear and apparel.

Next, the athlete may be asked to jog for a few minutes on a treadmill. Data about the run is recorded for analysis. Scientists can give athletes insight into their form. For example, the analysis can note whether runners lean forward too much or run on their toes. The experts can also make recommendations based on that analysis. For example, runners who lean forward too much may be able to run more efficiently by strengthening their hamstrings or glute muscles. Using data and testing, researchers can recommend the type of shoes best suited for specific athletes and their particular goals.

HIGH-TECH FACILITIES

Inside the NSRL, there is a full-size NBA regulation basketball court, a 200-meter running track, artificial training turf, and climate chambers. A wide variety of sensors track the activities in these facilities. These include 97 force plates, 400 motion capture cameras, and body-mapping equipment.

Underneath the track, turf, and basketball courts, force plates measure the force exerted when an athlete steps, jumps, or pushes off the ground. Unlike a scale that gives a single reading, the force plates gather data thousands of times per second in three dimensions: up and down, side to side, and back to front. For a runner on the track, the force plates measure the force each foot applies as it connects and pushes off the track surface.

On the track, force plates and motion capture cameras record data from sprints, long runs, and race starts. A 100-meter concrete strip re-creates outdoor running conditions. Athletes can also test different footwear. Nike collects data from runners at all levels that can be used to develop shoes appropriate for any runner, from a recreational jogger to an elite marathon runner.

At the Turf Lab, scientists can collect data on as many as 22 athletes. This is the number of players on the field during a soccer game. The players move at different speeds and in different directions. They interact with other players, their cleats, the ball, and the turf. Data about all

> *Courts, tracks, and fields at Nike's headquarters give employees a chance to test out the company's latest products.*

of these motions and interactions is recorded. The Turf Lab also has a screen where scientists project targets for athletes to aim at when going for a shot or passing the ball.

The Turf Lab has 200 cameras that capture movement. The data that scientists capture about an athlete's movement on the turf allows them to analyze how the tiniest design changes affect a product's performance. These findings can often apply beyond soccer to other field sports such as baseball, football, and rugby.

On the basketball court, motion capture cameras and force plates underneath the court surface capture similar data. Players wear sensors that track their heart rates and the speed of movement on the court. A force plate underneath the hoop records how a sneaker sole interacts with the court floor. Combined with the motion sensor tracking data, scientists can analyze how footwear affects speed and see how the sneaker sole interacts with the floor throughout the movements.

Inside Nike's climate chambers, technicians can control the temperature, humidity, and wind speed. They can even simulate the sun's radiant heat, imitating conditions ranging from the heat of the Sahara Desert to the frosty cold of Russia. They gather data about how athletes, apparel, and footwear perform under different conditions. Data from the climate chambers helps Nike designers determine which apparel and footwear features and designs will make

NIKE ADAPT

For athletes, getting the right shoe fit can be complicated. For example, a shoe that fits perfectly at the beginning of a basketball game may be uncomfortably tight in the third quarter after the foot expands a bit. To address this problem, Nike released a new self-lacing technology in the Nike Adapt BB basketball shoe in 2019. When a player puts on the shoe, a custom lacing system electronically adjusts to the shape of their foot and secures the foot through a range of movements. The self-lacing technology adjusts as needed. When the foot expands, the shoe loosens automatically. Players can also input different fit settings manually or by using a smartphone app.

garments more breathable and efficient in all types of weather. Sometimes, Nike researchers use life-size thermal mannequins that can sweat in the climate chambers. Using the mannequins allows researchers to test different environmental conditions without putting additional stress on actual humans.

Nike's commitment to research, design, and innovation has helped make it one of the leading athletic footwear and apparel companies globally. "The new products Nike is constantly innovating keeps the brand fresh and interesting for audiences," says branding expert and University of Southern California professor Jeetendr Sehdev. "It's why people of all ages want to wear Nike."[2]

DRI-FIT FABRIC

In apparel, Nike has created Dri-FIT technology to make sweating more comfortable. Dri-FIT is a polyester fabric designed to keep people wearing it dry so they can work longer and harder without becoming uncomfortable in wet clothes. Dri-FIT fabric's microfibers wick away sweat and spread it across the fabric's surface, allowing it to evaporate and dry faster. Dri-FIT mimics the body's natural cooling system, in which sweat evaporates and cools the skin.

CHAPTER EIGHT

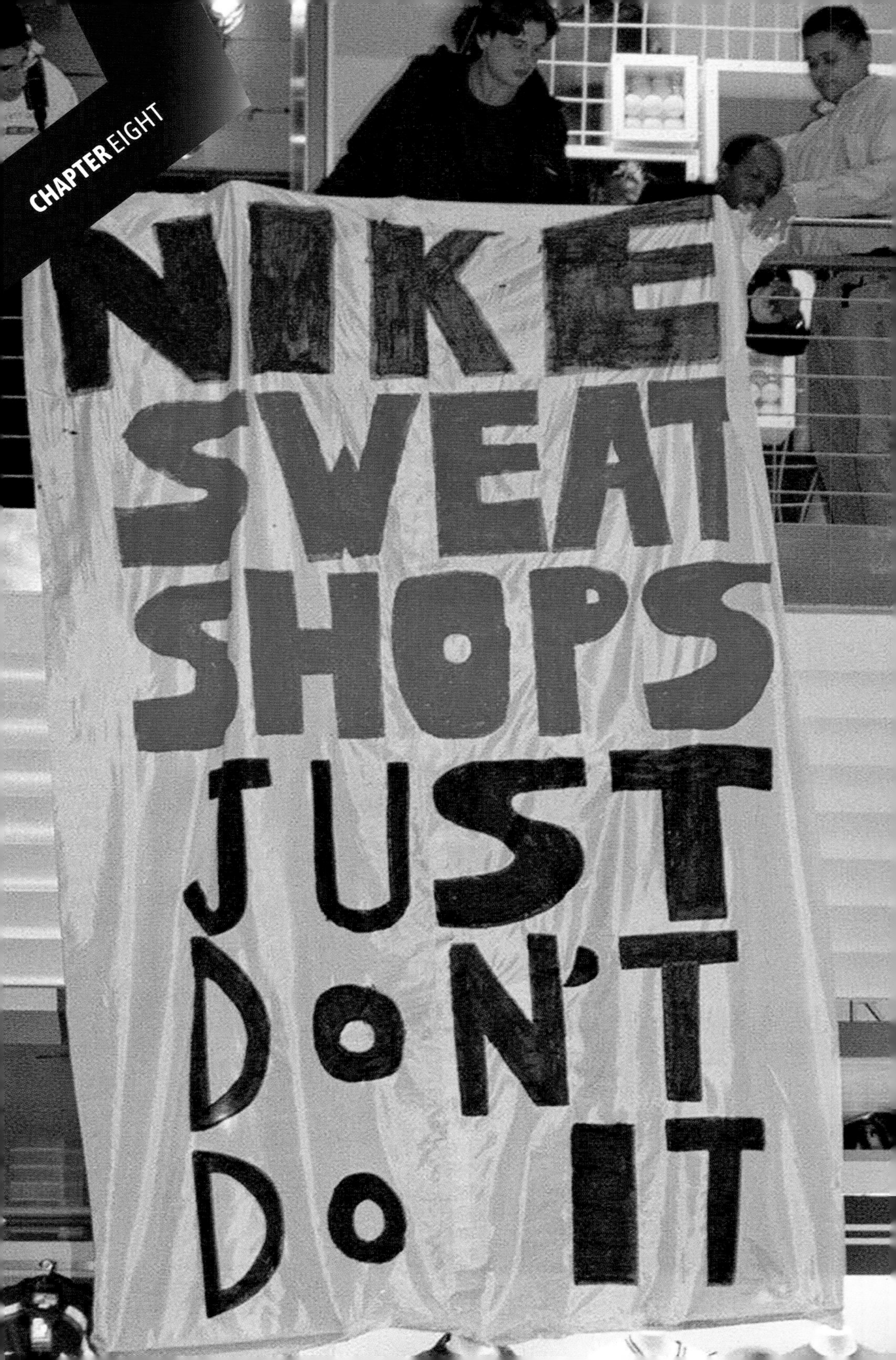

CONTROVERSIES

O ver the years, Nike has been involved in its share of controversies. Some controversies have involved the company's business practices. Other times, scandals involving some of Nike's athlete endorsers have caused negative publicity for the company.

SWEATSHOP SCANDAL

Nike has long outsourced the manufacturing of its products to factories in foreign countries. Before the 1990s, most of Nike's products were produced in South Korea and Taiwan. In these countries, workers earned very low wages, and Nike could produce its apparel and footwear very cheaply. When wages rose in Korea and

> *Many of Nike's controversies have centered on the ways in which its products are produced.*

77

> *Workers in a Vietnam factory assemble Nike shoes in 1997.*

Taiwan, Nike moved production to factories in Indonesia, China, and Vietnam. In these places, labor was cheaper. Because the cost of living varies around the world, a low wage in the United States may be a living wage overseas. Still, wages were sometimes extremely low even by those standards, and government officials sometimes did little to protect worker rights.

In 1991, activist Jeff Ballinger published a report about the poor conditions and low wages in many factories where Nike products were made. The report received a lot of attention from people in the United States and worldwide. People were shocked by reports of Indonesian workers earning as little as 14 cents an hour.[1] Allegations of child labor and abuse of factory workers surfaced. One story alleged that a subcontractor in Vietnam made female workers run laps to the point of exhaustion if they did not wear regulation shoes to work. Another report alleged that factory workers were forced to live in slums near open sewers. A magazine article included a picture of a 12-year-old Pakistani boy sewing a Nike soccer ball.

As these stories surfaced, many people criticized Nike for contracting with factories with known sweatshop conditions. Because Nike did not own or operate the overseas factories, Nike executives argued that the company was not responsible for what happened in these

WHAT IS A SWEATSHOP?

A sweatshop is a factory or other place of work where employees are forced to work in inhumane conditions. Sweatshop workers often earn very little. They are forced to work long hours and put themselves at risk in unsafe conditions. Some sweatshops use young children as workers. Sweatshops are usually found in developing countries such as Vietnam, Cambodia, Indonesia, Bangladesh, India, and Thailand. In these nations, labor laws may not be strictly enforced.

factories. However, many people did not accept this defense. Activists held public protests at Nike stores and the Olympics. Many customers began to boycott the brand.

By 1998, the ongoing scandal was seen as a factor in Nike's declining sales, and the company was forced to lay off some employees. Trust in Nike was falling among many of its consumers. "The sweatshop perception was one of the biggest challenges Nike has faced," said Jeetendr Sehdev. "It seemed impossible they could ever shake the perception."[2]

Finally, Nike cofounder Phil Knight took a stand against unfair and unsafe labor practices. He made changes within the company to address and improve the labor issues overseas. Nike raised the minimum wage paid to workers and strengthened its oversight of labor practices. "Nike admitted it wasn't perfect and that it was flawed. This gave it more credibility with consumers," said Sehdev.[3]

Nike published a report that revealed the conditions and pay in its overseas factories in an attempt to be transparent with the public. It created a complete list of factories that Nike contracted with and acknowledged many issues. Nike continues to publish public reports of conditions in its factories. Although Nike has made many improvements, a 2018 report by the Clean Clothes Campaign found that the company still paid poverty-level wages to some overseas workers.

COLIN KAEPERNICK CONTROVERSY

In 2018, Nike stirred more controversy when the company announced that former NFL quarterback Colin Kaepernick would be one of the athletes starring in new ads to celebrate the thirtieth anniversary of Nike's "Just Do It" slogan. In 2016, when Kaepernick was a quarterback for the San Francisco 49ers, he drew attention with his pregame protests. Kaepernick wanted to bring attention to police killings of Black Americans and other racial injustices in the United States. To do this, he knelt on one knee during the national anthem. Though

TREATMENT OF WOMEN

In May 2019, Olympic sprinter Allyson Felix wrote an op-ed in the *New York Times* that blasted Nike's treatment of the female athletes it sponsors. Felix revealed that when she was pregnant with her daughter in 2018, Nike attempted to cut her endorsement deal by as much as 70 percent.[4] The company said Felix would not be able to maintain her previous performance levels after giving birth. Felix and other female athletes with similar stories said they felt betrayed by Nike. Ultimately Felix left Nike and signed a deal with Athleta, a women-focused apparel company. She has also launched a shoe and lifestyle brand called Saysh. Nike later announced that it was changing its contracts for female athletes to include protections during pregnancy.

many supported Kaepernick's message, his gesture also sparked controversy. Some claimed that Kaepernick and other Black players who knelt during the national anthem were disrespectful to the American flag, the country, and military veterans. Emotions flared as people on both sides of the issue argued across the country. Kaepernick's contract with the 49ers was not renewed after 2016, and no other NFL team signed him. Kaepernick sued the NFL for allegedly conspiring to keep him out of the league, later settling the lawsuit in 2019.

Kaepernick could not get a job in the NFL, but Nike stood by its athlete. A Nike ad featured a black-and-white, close-up photo of Kaepernick with the words "Believe in something, even if it means sacrificing everything" written across the center of his face. The ad's wording was a clear reference to Kaepernick's lawsuit against the NFL. Gino Fisanotti, vice president of the Nike brand, announced the ad campaign and said, "We believe Colin is one of the most inspirational athletes of this generation, who has leveraged the power of sport to help move the world forward. We wanted to energize its meaning and introduce 'Just Do It' to a new generation of athletes."[5]

While it had many supporters, including Nike athletes LeBron James and Serena Williams, the ad campaign

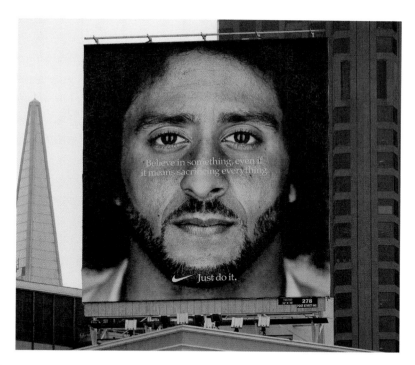

> Ads featuring Colin Kaepernick proved to be polarizing, attracting both critics and supporters.

sparked criticism. Opponents threatened to boycott Nike, and the hashtag #BoycottNike trended on Twitter. Some people posted images on social media of burning Nike shoes or cutting the Nike logo from their socks. Nike's share price dropped by 2 percent in a single day.[6]

Despite the controversy, some marketing experts believe that Nike made a wise decision with the Kaepernick ad. Ben Hayman, the managing partner of branding agency Given, said, "Ultimately, Nike has made a strategic decision about what matters to its core and future audience. As with any celebrity endorsement, it has aligned with an ambassador that represents its brand idea but critically connects that idea to its core target audience. . . . Overall the Nike campaign is a great move. It lights a fire under the brand, as well as the issue."[7]

HONG KONG PROTESTS

In 2019, Nike removed a line of products from China after a designer's social media posts supporting political protests in Hong Kong ignited controversy. In June of that year, protests erupted in Hong Kong over a controversial bill that would have allowed extradition from Hong Kong to China. Many people feared the proposed law could be used to deport activists from Hong Kong, which had long operated with its own judicial system. Although the bill was eventually suspended, disruptive protests persisted in the city.

The Nike shoes involved were designed by Undercover, a brand of Japanese designer Jun Takahashi.

STICKING WITH TIGER

Golfer Tiger Woods is one of Nike's most famous athlete endorsers. In 2009, reports that Woods had engaged in affairs with multiple women surfaced and seriously damaged his good-guy, family-man image. Several of Woods's corporate sponsors, including AT&T, Gatorade, *Golf Digest*, and Tag Heuer, dropped him because of the scandal. Nike, however, maintained its relationship with the golfer. They remained partners as Woods rebuilt his personal life, image, and career in the years since the scandal.

In June 2019, Undercover posted a photo of Hong Kong protesters on its Instagram account with the slogan "no extradition to China."[8] The post received a negative response from Chinese social media users. Undercover deleted the post, but the damage was done.

In response to Undercover's post, Chinese retailers stopped the sale of the limited-edition shoes. Based on feedback from Chinese consumers, Nike withdrew products designed by Undercover from China. Although the controversy had little impact on Nike's overall sales in China, it showed how difficult it could be for multinational companies to maneuver political disputes in the countries where they operate.

NIKE VAPORFLY DEBATE

In 2017, Nike introduced a new line of running shoes, the Nike Vaporfly. The shoe featured extra-thick soles and a springy carbon-fiber plate in the midsole designed so that a runner loses less energy with each step. Both Nike researchers and independent studies found that the shoes increased an athlete's energy efficiency by 4 percent or more. Over a marathon, 4 percent is significant. A person running at a 2-hour, 10-minute pace would see a 3.5-minute improvement in his time. That is a significant change for an elite marathon runner who earns prize money based on his finish.

The Vaporfly technology proved to be a game changer. Runners who wore the shoes turned in record-breaking times. In 2016, three medalists in the Summer Olympics in Rio de Janeiro, Brazil, all wore Vaporfly prototypes. In 2019, New York City Marathon winner Geoffrey Kamworor wore Vaporfly shoes for his winning time of 2 hours, 8 minutes, 13 seconds. In that year, 31 out of 36 podium finishers in the world's six biggest marathons wore Vaporflys.[9]

Some runners and scientists believed the shoes gave wearers an unfair advantage. The Vaporfly midsole acts like a spring, absorbing energy with each footfall and returning

THE OREGON PROJECT

In 2001, Nike launched the Oregon Project with the goal of making American distance runners more competitive. Led by head coach Alberto Salazar, the project recruited promising runners to live and train together in Oregon, near the Nike headquarters. Several runners turned in their best performances while on the team, including Olympic medalist Galen Rupp. However, in 2015, some former team members accused Salazar of encouraging runners to take unnecessary prescription medications to enhance performance. Also, a Nike scientist reported suspicious levels of the hormone testosterone in Oregon Project runners' blood tests. In 2019, the US Anti-Doping Agency announced a four-year ban of Salazar for trafficking of testosterone and tampering with the doping-control process. Ten days later, Nike announced that it was shutting down the Oregon Project.

> *The impressive performance of athletes wearing Nike's Vaporfly shoes raised questions about a potential unfair advantage.*

some of that stored energy to push the runner forward. "The runner runs the race, but the shoe enables him or her to run it faster for the same effort or ability," said Geoff Burns, a kinesiology researcher and professional runner. "So for two athletes of equal ability on race day, the one with the shoes is going to beat the one without the shoes."[10]

In 2020, the track-and-field governing body, World Athletics, ruled that runners could wear Vaporflys in competition, including in the Olympic Games. However, runners were not permitted to wear prototype shoes that had not been available to buy for at least four months. In addition, all shoes had to meet certain design specifications and not have a sole thicker than 40 millimeters [1.6 inches].[11] "It is not our job to regulate the entire sports shoe market, but it is our duty to preserve the integrity of elite competition by ensuring that the shoes worn by elite athletes in competition do not offer any unfair assistance or advantage," said Sebastian Coe, the president of World Athletics and a former Olympic track-and-field champion.[12]

NIKE ZOOM VAPORFLY 4%

I n 2017, Nike introduced the Nike Zoom Vaporfly 4%, a running shoe that promised to make wearers run faster. Nike even told consumers how much faster in the sneaker's name. The Zoom Vaporfly 4% features innovative technology for runners in its special ZoomX midsole foam and carbon fiber–plate insert. According to researchers, the curved carbon fiber plate stabilizes the ankle and reduces the work a runner's calves have to do, saving energy. The insert also keeps the runner's toes straight, which saves more energy. Finally, the ZoomX foam in the shoe's midsole squishes with each footfall and springs back to return some of the energy the foot applies with each step. Because the shoe's design saves energy, it allows the runner to run faster.

CHAPTER NINE

TEAMING UP TO DO GOOD

A s one of the world's most recognizable brands, Nike says that it is committed to a better world for all. John Donahoe, Nike president and chief executive officer, says, "Nike is a brand of hope and inspiration. We believe in the power of sport to bring out the best in people, and the potential of people to bring out the best in our world."[1] To work toward this goal, Nike has invested in programs and organizations that support people, the planet, and building community. Nike took its first steps into sustainability in 1993, when the company began grinding up old shoes and donating the material to builders of tracks, basketball courts, and other sports surfaces. This recycling

> *Workers in Portland apply and spread a layer of recycled Nike Grind rubber while building a new playing field.*

program continues today as Nike Grind. It collects leftover Nike manufacturing materials, such as scraps of rubber, foam, leather, textiles, and plastics. It also collects unsellable products and worn-out sneakers. Instead of being thrown away, these materials are processed into new substances that can be used in various ways.

Nike Grind materials are still being used for turf fields, running tracks, and other sports surfaces. More than 25 years after the first recycling program, sports surfaces made with Nike Grind materials can be found in more than 10,000 projects worldwide. In addition, Nike Grind materials are used in retail stores as part of many features, including wall and shelving displays, flooring, seating, mannequins, and modular display blocks. Some Nike products, including Nike and Converse footwear, are made with Nike Grind materials. Nike Grind materials are also being repurposed into apparel trim, such as zipper pulls, buttons, grommets, and cord locks. By 2021, more than 75 percent of all Nike apparel and shoes contained recycled materials.[2]

REDUCING WASTE

Nike Grind is just one part of Nike's overall goal to reduce waste across its business and products. Toward this end, the company has created several tools that help its product design team reduce waste, starting with a product's initial design. For example, Nike's Materials Sustainability Index is a score based on the energy, water, and chemicals used to make materials, along with the waste generated in the manufacturing process. There are also product scores for footwear and apparel, which evaluate the waste generated during manufacturing based on the product's design. Together, these sustainability scores give product-development teams the information to reduce the resources used and waste generated by Nike products.

In Nike manufacturing facilities, offices, and distribution centers, reducing waste is a priority. More than half of footwear waste in factories is recycled and either used or sold to other businesses. At Nike distribution centers, cardboard

NIKE REFURBISHED

The Nike Refurbished program is one of the company's key programs to reduce waste. When a customer returns a pair of shoes to Nike, the Nike Refurbished team inspects and repairs the shoes. The team uses a variety of tools and products to get the shoes as close to new as possible. Once the repair work is completed, the team assigns the shoes a condition grade. The refurbished shoes can then be priced based on their condition grade and resold to customers. In 2021, Nike Refurbished was available in several US Nike stores, with plans to expand into more locations.

shipping boxes are being recycled and reused. The company is also testing other packing ideas, such as reusable shipping totes. In company offices, employees are encouraged to compost, recycle, and reduce waste. At Nike headquarters in Oregon, a reusable dishware program eliminates the need for to-go boxes.

MOVE TO ZERO

In 2019, Nike announced a new sustainability initiative called Move to Zero. The plan built upon existing company programs to reduce waste and carbon emissions. "At Nike, we believe that climate change is the defining environmental issue of our generation because the reality is if there's no planet, there's no sport. And as you might imagine sports are fairly important to us," said Chief Sustainability Officer Noel Kinder.[3]

In addition to the company's waste reduction programs, Move to Zero sets ambitious

POWERED WITH RENEWABLE ENERGY

In Ham, Belgium, a Nike distribution center gets its power from 100 percent renewable energy. The distribution center uses energy generated from local wind, solar, geothermal, hydroelectric, and biomass energy sources. Also, because the distribution center is located near a network of canals, 99 percent of inbound containers arrive at the facility via water. Using the canals eliminates approximately 14,000 truck routes annually and reduces carbon emissions related to truck operations.[4]

targets for Nike to reduce its carbon footprint by 2030. The company aimed to reduce emissions by between 30 and 65 percent by 2030. In North America, Nike powers its owned or operated facilities with 100 percent renewable energy. This transition brought the company one step closer to its goal of using 100 percent renewable energy in all its owned or operated facilities worldwide.[5] Nike is also encouraging the adoption of renewable energy through its entire supply chain.

INVESTING IN PLAY

Research shows that active kids are healthier, more confident, and more successful in school and life. However, only one in five kids worldwide gets the physical activity they need. Some kids face more barriers to play than others. To give all kids the opportunity to be active and play sports, Nike has made a global commitment to getting kids moving, regardless of background, gender identity, ability, or goals.

Nike works with local partners to increase participation in sports, particularly for girls and kids from marginalized communities. For example, Nike announced an initiative with the NFL in 2021 that will provide $5 million in products to support girls' flag football high school programs.[6] In addition to the grant, Nike is also adapting its online football training series to include content designed for flag football athletes. The training will include how-to drills, training education, team building, and leadership development instruction.

Nike is also working to help communities train new coaches. Good coaches are essential to getting kids excited about and participating in sports. The company has partnered with the US Olympic & Paralympic Committee and the Aspen Institute Project Play to create free online training tools to help coaches give all children positive experiences in sports. Together with local partners, Nike aims to train coaches and make sports more accessible for all.

BUILDING COMMUNITY

In the community, Nike invests in programs and organizations to build more inclusive and active communities. In 2020, Nike, Converse, Jordan Brand, and Michael Jordan partnered and committed $140 million over ten years to support organizations working to address racial inequality for Black Americans.[7] Nike's community investment program, called Until We All Win, is also committed to diversity and inclusion. The program

> *Nike's charity and community-building programs are aimed at helping the next generation of athletes.*

awards $5 million in grants to nonprofit organizations that work in underrepresented communities in cities where Nike's employees and customers have strong relationships. With these grants, Nike strives to make a difference for marginalized people.

Nike also supports its employees in their efforts to improve the communities where they live and work. The Nike Community Impact Fund supports local, grassroots organizations that encourage kids to get active and make a positive impact through play. Employees award grants to local nonprofits and schools. Nike also supports its employees' hands-on efforts in the community. Through the company's Give Your Best program, Nike matches employee donations to schools and other nonprofit organizations. When employees volunteer, they earn a $10 credit per volunteer hour, up to $2,500 per year. The employee can then direct Nike to donate those funds to the organization of their choosing. Nike has donated millions of dollars to more than 2,000 organizations worldwide through this program, supporting racial and social justice, education, environmental causes, COVID-19 relief efforts, and more.[8]

NIKE COMMUNITY AMBASSADORS

Through its Community Ambassador program, Nike encourages its store employees to share their love of sports with local youth. In fiscal year 2020, Nike trained more than 6,700 employees from stores in 29 countries to become volunteer youth coaches in their communities. During the year, these employees volunteered more than 60,000 hours.[9] Through their hands-on efforts, Nike employees are helping local youth stay active and participate in sports.

BUILDING THE NIKE BRAND

Nike's dedication to innovation has helped it grow from a small shoe distributor into one of the best-known companies in the world. The company attracts and retains loyal customers through top-quality shoes, apparel, and other products. Nike's brand is broad enough that it can cater to both elite athletes and everyday people.

Yet product innovation is only one part of Nike's success. Over the years, the company has become a master at marketing to and engaging with customers. "For years, we thought of ourselves as a production-oriented company, meaning we put all our emphasis on designing and manufacturing the product," said founder Phil Knight. "But now we understand that the most important thing we do is market the product."[10]

ESSENTIAL FACTS

KEY EVENTS

- In 1964, Phil Knight and Bill Bowerman start an athletic-shoe distribution company called Blue Ribbon Sports.

- In 1972, Blue Ribbon Sports launches a line of athletic shoes under the brand name Nike.

- Blue Ribbon Sports officially changes its name to Nike Inc. in 1978 and introduces the Nike Tailwind running shoe. It is the first athletic shoe to incorporate air technology into the soles.

- In December 1980, Nike issues two million shares of stock in a public offering.

- Nike establishes its first research lab in 1980 in Exeter, New Hampshire. The research lab located at company headquarters in Beaverton, Oregon, is where today's Nike scientists and designers study and create the latest shoe and apparel technology.

- Nike signs promising young basketball player Michael Jordan to an endorsement deal in 1984.

- In 1988, Nike launches its iconic "Just Do It" slogan and marketing campaign.

- In 2018, Nike stirs controversy when it features former NFL quarterback and activist Colin Kaepernick in a new marketing campaign.

- In 2020, *Forbes* magazine ranks Nike number 13 on its listing of the most valuable brands in the world.

KEY PEOPLE

- Phil Knight is the cofounder of Nike. He led the company for several decades before retiring in 2016.

- Bill Bowerman cofounds Nike with Phil Knight. Bowerman was a track-and-field coach who was responsible for several of Nike's early design innovations, including the Waffle Trainer.

- M. Frank Rudy, a former aerospace engineer, and his business partner, Bob Bogert, develop the air technology used in many Nike sneakers.

- Michael Jordan is a legendary basketball player who signed a major endorsement deal with Nike. His Jordan Brand line of products generates billions of dollars in sales for Nike each year.

KEY PRODUCTS

- Air Force 1: This 1982 basketball sneaker, designed by Nike product designer Bruce Kilgore, has become Nike's best-selling sneaker of all time.

- Air Jordan 1: Introduced in 1985, this was the first sneaker release in a long and profitable partnership between basketball star Michael Jordan and Nike.

- Air Max 1: This 1987 running sneaker was the first sneaker to feature visible air technology.

- Nike Zoom Vaporfly 4%: This running sneaker, released in 2017, has been shown to make wearers run faster.

QUOTE

"Nike is a brand of hope and inspiration. We believe in the power of sport to bring out the best in people, and the potential of people to bring out the best in our world."

—John Donahoe, Nike president and chief executive officer, 2021

GLOSSARY

apparel
A synonym for clothes.

baseline
A starting point used for comparison.

boycott
To refuse to have dealings with, usually in order to express disapproval or to force acceptance of certain conditions.

brand
A name or mark a company uses to distinguish its products from those of other companies.

distribution
Supplying goods to stores and other businesses that sell to consumers.

endorsement
A public recommendation or suggestion to use a certain product.

force
A push or pull on an object resulting from the object's interaction with another object.

innovative

Featuring original new methods and features.

logo

A simple design appearing on products and advertising that represents a company.

midsole

A layer of material between the inner and outer soles of a shoe that absorbs shock.

polyester

A synthetic fabric used in clothing and shoes.

sensor

A device that detects or measures a physical property.

slogan

A short and striking or memorable phrase used in advertising.

sustainability

Meeting current needs without harming the ability of future generations to meet their needs.

ADDITIONAL RESOURCES

SELECTED BIBLIOGRAPHY

Golden, Jessica. "How Phil Knight Turned a Dream into a $25 Billion Fortune." *CNBC*, 9 May 2016, *cnbc.com*. Accessed 25 Jan. 2022.

Knight, Phil. *Shoe Dog*. Simon & Schuster, 2016.

Witte, Rae. "How Nike Innovates for Everyday Athletes." *TechCrunch*, 26 Oct. 2021, techcrunch.com. Accessed 25 Jan. 2022.

FURTHER READINGS

Knight, Phil. *Shoe Dog (Young Readers Edition)*. Simon & Schuster, 2019.

Steffens, Bradley. *The Science and Technology of Basketball*. ReferencePoint, 2020.

Streissguth, Tom. *Adidas*. Abdo, 2023.

ONLINE RESOURCES

To learn more about Nike, please visit **abdobooklinks.com** or scan this QR code. These links are routinely monitored and updated to provide the most current information available.

MORE INFORMATION

For more information on this subject, contact or visit the following organizations:

NIKE NYC
650 5th Ave.
New York, NY 10019
212-376-9480
nike.com/retail/s/nike-nyc-house-of-innovation-000

Nike's flagship store in New York City fills six stories and is a place where sports lovers can go and play in an experience-driven retail facility.

NIKE WORLD HEADQUARTERS
1 Bowerman Dr.
Beaverton, OR 97005
503-671-6453
jobs.nike.com/whq

The Nike World Headquarters, a massive complex containing dozens of buildings, is located in Oregon.

SPORT MARKETING ASSOCIATION
1972 Clark Ave.
Alliance, OH 44601
330-823-4054
sportmarketingassociation.com

Founded in 2002, the Sport Marketing Association aims to develop and expand the body of knowledge in sport marketing.

SOURCE NOTES

CHAPTER 1. HOT NEW RELEASE

1. "Nike, Inc. Reports Fiscal 2021 Fourth Quarter and Full Year Results." *Nike*, 24 June 2021, investors.nike.com. Accessed 23 Feb. 2022.

2. "#13 Nike." *Forbes*, 2022, forbes.com. Accessed 23 Feb. 2022.

3. "Fun Facts about the Nike Headquarters in Portland." *Provenance Hotels*, 2022, provenancehotels.com. Accessed 23 Feb. 2022.

4. D. Tighe. "Total Nike Retail Stores Worldwide from 2009 to 2021." *Statista*, 2022, statista.com. Accessed 23 Feb. 2022.

5. Marty Swant. "The World's Most Valuable Brands." *Forbes*, 2022, forbes.com. Accessed 23 Feb. 2022.

CHAPTER 2. IN THE BEGINNING

1. Emmie Martin. "How Phil Knight Built Nike into One of the Biggest Brands in the World and Became a Billionaire." *Business Insider*, 23 Aug. 2015, businessinsider.com. Accessed 23 Feb. 2022.

2. Pratiti Soumya. "The Story of NIKE—Sports, Enthusiasm, Advertising Legend." *Medium*, 22 Aug. 2017, medium.com. Accessed 23 Feb. 2022.

3. "Nike, Inc. History." *Funding Universe*, n.d., fundinguniverse.com. Accessed 23 Feb. 2022.

4. Jessica Golden. "How Phil Knight Turned a Dream into a $25 Billion Fortune." *CNBC*, 9 May 2016, cnbc.com. Accessed 23 Feb. 2022.

5. Tracy Carbasho. *Nike*. ABC-CLIO, 2010. 186.

6. "40 Years of Prefontaine." *Nike News*, 1 June 2015, news.nike.com. Accessed 23 Feb. 2022.

CHAPTER 3. EXPANSION AND GROWTH

1. Phil Knight. *Shoe Dog*. Simon & Schuster, 2016. 199.

2. Knight, *Shoe Dog*, 215.

3. "Nike, Inc. History." *Funding Universe*, n.d., fundinguniverse.com. Accessed 23 Feb. 2022.

4. Knight, *Shoe Dog*, 284.

5. Knight, *Shoe Dog*, 313.

6. Knight, *Shoe Dog*, 313.

7. Knight, *Shoe Dog*, 306.

8. Kate Vinton. "Nike Cofounder and Chairman Phil Knight Officially Retires from the Board." *Forbes*, 30 June 2016, forbes.com. Accessed 23 Feb. 2022.

CHAPTER 4. A MARKETING MASTER

1. "Betting on a Legend—The Story of Nike's Air Jordan Shoe." *Young Investors Society*, n.d., yis.org. Accessed 23 Feb. 2022.

2. Zack Schlemmer. "Jordan 101: The One That Started It All." *Sneaker News*, 11 June 2015, sneakernews.com. Accessed 23 Feb. 2022.

3. "Legends Profile: Michael Jordan." *NBA History*, 14 Sept. 2021, nba.com. Accessed 23 Feb. 2022.

4. Darren Rovell. "How Nike Landed Michael Jordan." *ESPN*, 15 Feb. 2013, espn.com. Accessed 23 Feb. 2022.

5. "Ad Campaigns: Just Do It." *San Francisco School of Copywriting*, n.d., sanfranciscoschoolofcopywriting.com. Accessed 23 Feb. 2022.

6. Tracy Carbasho. *Nike*. ABC-CLIO, 2010. 262.

7. Allan Brettman. "Nike, Wieden + Kennedy Women's Ad Campaign Broke New Ground 20 Years Ago." *Oregon Live*, 9 Jan. 2019, oregonlive.com. Accessed 23 Feb. 2022.

SOURCE NOTES CONTINUED

CHAPTER 5. PROMOTING NIKE

1. Chris Isidore. "How Nike Became King of Endorsements." *CNN Money*, 5 June 2015, money.cnn.com. Accessed 23 Feb. 2022.

2. Laura Woods. "Why Nike Uses Endorsements & Sponsorships." *Bizfluent*, 26 Sept. 2017, bizfluent.com. Accessed 23 Feb. 2022.

3. Haresh Ramchandani. "40 Incredible Stats as Serena Williams Turns 40." *Tennis Majors*, 26 September 2021, tennismajors.com. Accessed 23 Feb. 2022.

4. Weston Blasi. "When LeBron James Chose Nike in 2003, He Gave Up $28 Million." *MarketWatch*, 1 Sept. 2019, marketwatch.com. Accessed 23 Feb. 2022.

5. Ahiza Garcia. "NFL and Nike Sign 8-Year Contract for Uniforms." *CNN Money*, 27 Mar. 2018, money.cnn.com. Accessed 23 Feb. 2022.

6. Liam Fox. "Nike Brand Profile & Strategy." *Sportcal*, 1 July 2020, sportcal.com. Accessed 23 Feb. 2022.

CHAPTER 6. NIKE'S FAMILY OF PRODUCTS

1. D. Tighe. "Revenue Share of Nike Worldwide in 2021, by Product Category." *Statista*, 2022, statista.com. Accessed 23 Feb. 2022.

2. Tighe, "Revenue Share of Nike Worldwide."

3. Tighe, "Revenue Share of Nike Worldwide."

4. "Apple & Nike Launch the Perfect Running Partner, Apple Watch Nike+." *Apple*, 7 Sept. 2016, apple.com. Accessed 23 Feb. 2022.

5. Peter Verry. "How Nike Became So Popular." *Footwear News*, 30 Sept. 2020, footwearnews.com. Accessed 23 Feb. 2022.

6. D. Tighe. "Total Nike Retail Stores Worldwide from 2009 to 2021." *Statista*, 2022, statista.com. Accessed 23 Feb. 2022.

7. Stephanie Crets. "Nike's Q4 Online Sales Jump More than 50%." *Digital Commerce 360*, 1 July 2021, digitalcommerce360.com. Accessed 23 Feb. 2022.

8. Crets, "Nike's Q4 Online Sales Jump More than 50%."

9. Crets, "Nike's Q4 Online Sales Jump More than 50%."

CHAPTER 7. HIGH-TECH DESIGN

1. "Meet the LeBron James Innovation Center." *Nike*, 4 Oct. 2021, news.nike.com. Accessed 23 Feb. 2022.

2. Ashley Lutz. "How Nike Shed Its Sweatshop Image to Dominate the Shoe Industry." *Business Insider*, 6 June 2015, businessinsider.com. Accessed 23 Feb. 2022.

CHAPTER 8. CONTROVERSIES

1. Ashley Lutz. "How Nike Shed Its Sweatshop Image to Dominate the Shoe Industry." *Business Insider*, 6 June 2015, businessinsider.com. Accessed 23 Feb. 2022.

2. Lutz, "How Nike Shed Its Sweatshop Image."

3. Lutz, "How Nike Shed Its Sweatshop Image."

4. Kelly McLaughlin and Meredith Cash. "Olympian Allyson Felix Says Nike Was 'Beyond Disrespectful.'" *Insider*, 8 July 2021, insider.com. Accessed 23 Feb. 2022.

5. Martha Kelner. "Nike's Controversial Colin Kaepernick Ad Campaign Its Most Divisive Yet." *Guardian*, 4 Sept. 2018, theguardian.com. Accessed 23 Feb. 2022.

6. Kelner, "Nike's Controversial Colin Kaepernick Ad Campaign Its Most Divisive Yet."

7. Ben Hayman. "Why Nike Was Right to Feature Colin Kaepernick in Its Controversial New Ad." *Reuters Events*, 17 Sept. 2018, reutersevents.com. Accessed 23 Feb. 2022.

8. Yen Nee Lee. "Nike Pulled a Shoe Line from China after Its Designer Supported Hong Kong Protests." *CNBC*, 26 June 2019, cnbc.com. Accessed 23 Feb. 2022.

9. Aylin Woodward. "Nike's Controversial Vaporfly Shoes Are Helping Runners Set New Records, but Some Think It's 'Technology Doping.' Here's How They Work." *Business Insider*, 16 Jan. 2020, businessinsider.com. Accessed 23 Feb. 2022.

10. Woodward, "Nike's Controversial Vaporfly Shoes."

11. Matthew Futterman. "Nike Vaporfly Shoes Avoid Olympics Ban." *New York Times*, 31 Jan. 2020, nytimes.com. Accessed 23 Feb. 2022.

12. Futterman, "Nike Vaporfly Shoes Avoid Olympics Ban."

CHAPTER 9. TEAMING UP TO DO GOOD

1. "FY20 Nike Inc. Impact Report: Breaking Barriers." *Nike*, n.d., nike.com. Accessed 23 Feb. 2022.

2. Noel Kinder. "Our Carbon Footprint and Our Next Steps." *Nike News*, 13 Apr. 2021, news.nike.com. Accessed 23 Feb. 2022.

3. John Balkam. "A Common Purpose for Sports." *Win-Win-Win*, 20 Feb. 2020, winwinwin.substack.com. Accessed 23 Feb. 2022.

4. "Carbon & Energy." *Nike*, n.d., purpose.nike.com. Accessed 23 Feb. 2022.

5. "Carbon & Energy."

6. "Nike Partners with the NFL to Grow Girls Flag Football in the U.S." *Play Football*, 2 Feb. 2021, playfootball.nfl.com. Accessed 23 Feb. 2022.

7. "Inclusive Communities." *Nike*, n.d., purpose.nike.com. Accessed 23 Feb. 2022.

8. "Employee Community Engagement." *Nike*, n.d., purpose.nike.com. Accessed 23 Feb. 2022.

9. "Employee Community Engagement."

10. Geraldine E. Willigan. "High-Performance Marketing: An Interview with Nike's Phil Knight." *Harvard Business Review*, July–Aug. 1992, hbr.org. Accessed 23 Feb. 2022.

INDEX

ABOUT THE AUTHOR

CARLA MOONEY

Carla Mooney is a graduate of the University of Pennsylvania with a degree in economics. Today, she writes for young people and is the author of many books for young adults and children. Mooney enjoys reading about business, marketing, and innovation. She also owns several pairs of Nike sneakers.

ABOUT THE CONSULTANT

MARK S. NAGEL

Mark S. Nagel is a faculty member in the Department of Sport and Entertainment Management at the University of South Carolina. He also regularly guest lectures at other colleges and universities. Before pursuing a career in academe, Nagel worked in different areas of sport management—primarily in athletic coaching and administration as well as campus recreation. During his years as an assistant coach of the women's basketball team at the University of San Francisco, he helped lead the team to three NCAA Tournament appearances and a spot in the 1996 Sweet 16.

Nagel has coauthored multiple textbooks including *Developing Successful Sport Marketing Plans* and *Developing Successful Sport Sponsorship Plans* as well as multiple editions of *Introduction to Sport Management: Theory and Practice, Financial Management in the Sport Industry*, and *Sport Facility Management: Organizing Events and Mitigating Risks*. In addition, he has published extensively in professional journals, written numerous academic book chapters, given dozens of research presentations, and served as a consultant on a variety of legal and management projects.